WE
THE PEOPLE
ELIZABETH
BLACKWELL

Library of Congress Cataloging-in-Publication Data

Klingel, Cynthia Fitterer.
  Elizabeth Blackwell.

  (We the people)
  Summary: A biography of Elizabeth Blackwell who over-
came many difficulties to become the first woman physician
in the United States.
  1. Blackwell, Elizabeth, 1821-1910—Juvenile
literature.   2. Physicians—New York (States)—Biography—
Juvenile literature.   3. Women physicians—New York
(State)—Biography—Juvenile literature.   [1. Blackwell,
Elizabeth, 1821-1910.   2. Women physicians.   3. Physicians]
I. Title.   II. Series: We the people (Mankato, Minn.)
R154.B623K58   1987   610.92′4   [B]   [92]   87-27153
ISBN 0-88682-169-X

WE
THE PEOPLE
ELIZABETH BLACKWELL

PIONEER DOCTOR
(1821-1910)

CINDY KLINGEL

Illustrated By John Nelson

CREATIVE EDUCATION

ELIZABETH BLACKWELL

Little Elizabeth crouched by the upstairs window. Outside, a riot was raging. Shouting men roamed the streets of Bristol, England. Burning buildings lit up the night sky. Elizabeth was afraid.

Later that day, her father came home and tried to explain why the riot had happened. "Poor people are hungry. They feel our government is unfair to them, and they think their only hope is to fight back with violence."

Elizabeth felt badly for these people who were unhappy. She wished that she could do something to help them. But she was young, and there really was nothing she could do.

Samuel Blackwell was a rich sugar merchant. His family did not suffer from poverty like many of the people who were upset with the government. But Samuel Blackwell was a compassionate man. He wished to help the suffering poor, but he

did not know how. His nine children shared his beliefs and tried to think of ways to help people who were more unfortunate than they were.

Before too long, the Blackwell family found out what it was like to be poor. Mr. Blackwell's business failed. He thought about his family and tried to decide what would be the best for them. Finally, he reached a decision. He said, "We will go to America and start over again."

Elizabeth was excited, but she was also very frightened to leave England. Elizabeth clung to the hand of her little sister, Emily, as they got on board a sailing ship. She tried to be brave as the shore of England disappeared and gray waves surged all around them.

The poorest passengers, deep in the ship's hold, took sick. Several died. Elizabeth watched with horror as the bodies were brought up, prayed over, and dropped into the sea. Her father said, "They died because they were poor. They had to travel in a dark, filthy hold. All over the world, people die needlessly because they are poor. Somehow, we must find a way to help them." Eleven-year-old Elizabeth nodded. She decided that someday she would try to help poor people who were sick and needed attention.

Mr. Blackwell started a new sugar business in New York. But he did not like the way the Americans made money in the sugar industry. He did not like to see slaves working in the cane fields.

"Black slaves deserve to be free!" said Blackwell. "How can I carry on a business that is founded upon human misery?" But it was the only business he knew. Once more he failed to prosper. In 1837, he took the family to Cincinnati, Ohio, hoping to make a fortune there. But his dreams did not come true, as he died shortly after they arrived in Ohio.

Elizabeth could no longer stay home. The family needed money to live on. So, at age sixteen, she went to work. Unlike most well-to-do young women of the time, she had been well educated. She became a teacher in Kentucky. Despite her youth, she was forceful and determined to succeed.

Elizabeth was impatient when men talked about how "inferior" women were. She knew women could do many things just as well as men could. Women did not have as many opportunities as men had. Women could not receive good educations and good jobs like the men could. Elizabeth felt women were being treated unfairly. She, like many other women of that time, was becoming aware of women's rights.

Was not one of those rights the right to earn a good living? Elizabeth thought so. Even the best woman teacher earned far less than a man. Wasn't her mind as good as that of any man she knew? Of course it was! If only men would give women a chance to prove themselves!

Several years went by. Elizabeth grew more and more frustrated. Although she was still young, she felt she was wasting her life. Then, when she was twenty-four years old, she happened to visit a friend named Mary who was dying. Elizabeth stayed for awhile and helped care for Mary. She enjoyed doing things to make Mary feel better and more comfortable.

Mary enjoyed having Elizabeth with her. Elizabeth was always gentle and kind. One day, Mary took Elizabeth's hand. "The worst of my illness is being treated by a gruff, unfeeling doctor. If only there were women doctors!"

Elizabeth agreed. Then her friend said, "You are young and strong. You could become a doctor."

Elizabeth thought about Mary's suggestion. Yes, thought Elizabeth, I would like to be a doctor. It would be a way of truly helping other people. But this was impossible! Women did not become doctors. However, Elizabeth could not forget her dying friend's words. For weeks she thought about it. Then she announced to her family, "I am going to try to become a doctor."

Her family was surprised, but very supportive. Elizabeth knew it would be very difficult. She wrote letters to doctors, asking for advice. Very few doctors replied, but they all told her she must go to medical school.

Elizabeth had great difficulty finding a place to study. She wrote letters to many different schools, but no medical school would admit a woman. So she studied privately at first, helped by Quaker doctors who believed in women's rights.

Finally, in 1847, she decided to try again. She applied to Geneva Medical College, a small school in New York. The student body voted, and as a joke, the school admitted her. They were all sure that Elizabeth could never keep up. The teachers and students waited for her to make a fool of herself and quit.

In those days, "nice" women fainted at the sight of blood. They never talked about the workings of the body. But Elizabeth was not silly.

Instead, she was brave and determined. She felt she could learn anything a man could learn—and she proved it. On exams, she consistently outscored the other students. Students who had laughed at her began to respect her courage and her fine mind. The jokes stopped. But Elizabeth was still an outsider because she seemed different from the other women. The townspeople of Geneva were sure she was some kind of indecent woman.

No one in town would speak to her. Elizabeth wished this were not so. She tried not to let it make her unhappy.

Hoping to learn even more, she helped treat the sick at Philadelphia's huge Blockley Almshouse during her summer vacation. The most miserable of the sick poor came to this place. Although she had learned a lot in her studies at Geneva Medical College, Elizabeth found out how truly ignorant she was as she tried to help the patients. "I must learn more!" she said. "There is so much work to be done among the sick. Somehow, I must get other women to help me."

That fall, she returned to school. At that time, a medical degree required only a short period of study. Elizabeth Blackwell became a doctor of medicine on January 23, 1849. She was the first woman physician to graduate in the United States.

She went to Paris to learn more

about the diseases of women and children. While treating a sick baby, she was infected with an eye disease. It caused her to lose the sight of one eye.

She needed a lot of courage in the weeks that followed. She suffered pain and self-doubt as well.

She went to England and became a friend of the famous nurse, Florence Nightingale. In 1850, she received good news. Lydia Folger had become the first American-born woman doctor, and now other women were seeking medical degrees. Even Emily, Elizabeth's younger sister, wanted to become a doctor.

Elizabeth realized that because she had worked hard and succeeded

in becoming a doctor, other women could now realize their dreams more easily.

The following year, in 1851, Dr. Elizabeth Blackwell returned to New York. Her great desire was to help the poor people who were sick but couldn't afford medical treatment. At first, she was not able to practice medicine. People were still very prejudiced against a woman doctor. They would not even rent her space to have an office.

Little by little, women patients came to her. She became used to their saying, "Why, you are a proper doctor after all!"

In 1853, she opened a dispensary, a kind of clinic, for treating poor women and children. She was joined in this work by her sister Emily, who graduated from medical school the following year. The two women begged their wealthy friends to help them start a real hospital.

Elizabeth and Emily Blackwell's dream came true in 1857, when the New York Infirmary for Women and Children opened its doors. It was the first true hospital anywhere in the world which was for women, run by women doctors.

Not only did the hospital treat the poor, but it also trained nurses. A black woman doctor, Rebecca Cole, joined the staff and set up the first "visiting doctor" service ever known in a large American city.

In 1868, the Infirmary opened its own medical college for women.

Then Elizabeth received a letter from England, begging her to come there and "do for the women of England what you have done in America." In 1869 she left the Infirmary in the capable hands of Emily and returned to the land of her birth. There she lived and worked for another 40 years. She continued as a champion of women's rights until her death on May 31, 1910.

Americans continue to remember Elizabeth Blackwell. In 1949, the Blackwell Medal was established to recognize women physicians who show achievement in the field of medicine. Elizabeth's perseverance and determination to succeed helped women after her to realize their dreams, too.

WE THE PEOPLE SERIES

WOMEN OF AMERICA

CLARA BARTON
JANE ADDAMS
ELIZABETH BLACKWELL
HARRIET TUBMAN
SUSAN B. ANTHONY
DOLLEY MADISON

INDIANS OF AMERICA

GERONIMO
CRAZY HORSE
CHIEF JOSEPH
PONTIAC
SQUANTO
OSCEOLA

FRONTIERSMEN OF AMERICA

DANIEL BOONE
BUFFALO BILL
JIM BRIDGER
FRANCIS MARION
DAVY CROCKETT
KIT CARSON

WAR HEROES OF AMERICA

JOHN PAUL JONES
PAUL REVERE
ROBERT E. LEE
ULYSSES S. GRANT
SAM HOUSTON
LAFAYETTE

EXPLORERS OF AMERICA

COLUMBUS
LEIF ERICSON
DeSOTO
LEWIS AND CLARK
CHAMPLAIN
CORONADO